How's the
Weather?

T0343968

Rob Waring, *Series Editor*

Australia · Canada · Mexico · Singapore · United Kingdom · United States

Words to Know

This story is about Earth's **atmosphere** and the **weather conditions** that occur there.

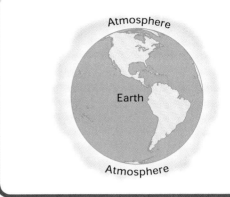

 Earth and Its Weather. Here are some kinds of weather you will find in the story. Label the pictures with words from the box.

hail	snowstorm	tornado
sandstorm	thunderstorm	typhoon

1. _____

2. _____

3. _____

4. _____

5. _____

6. _____

B **Predicting the Weather.** Read the paragraph. Complete the sentences with the correct form of the underlined words.

> Predicting the weather on the planet is a science known as <u>meteorology</u>. <u>Meteorologists</u> study the earth's atmosphere. Moving air masses in the atmosphere, or <u>fronts</u>, often cause changes in the weather. Meteorologists use devices such as <u>thermometers</u>, <u>radar</u>, and <u>satellites</u> to make <u>predictions</u> about fronts and other weather factors. They always want to be accurate. Many people listen to the weather <u>forecast</u> to plan their day.

1. A _____ is a scientist who studies the earth's atmosphere.

2. A _____ is a statement about what will happen in the future.

3. _____ is a system that uses radio waves to locate an object.

4. _____ is the study of the earth's atmosphere and weather.

5. A _____ is a line where warm and cold air masses meet.

6. A weather _____ tells what will happen with the weather.

7. A _____ is a device that measures the temperature of the air.

8. A _____ is a piece of equipment that sends and receives signals in space.

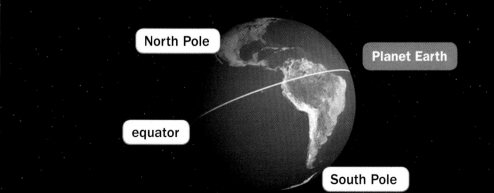

North Pole

Planet Earth

equator

South Pole

Look outside your window. It may be very different from what you saw just a day or two ago. Yesterday may have been cloudy and rainy, today may be beautiful and sunny. But what about tomorrow? Well, you may just want to stay inside!

What is it that causes these changes? It's the weather. The weather is something which we experience every day, and yet it's very complicated. The weather is the temporary state of the earth's atmosphere. It can be very different from place to place at any one time. This is because it depends on the complex relationship between the air, water, and heat from the sun.

How does the weather work?

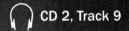 CD 2, Track 9

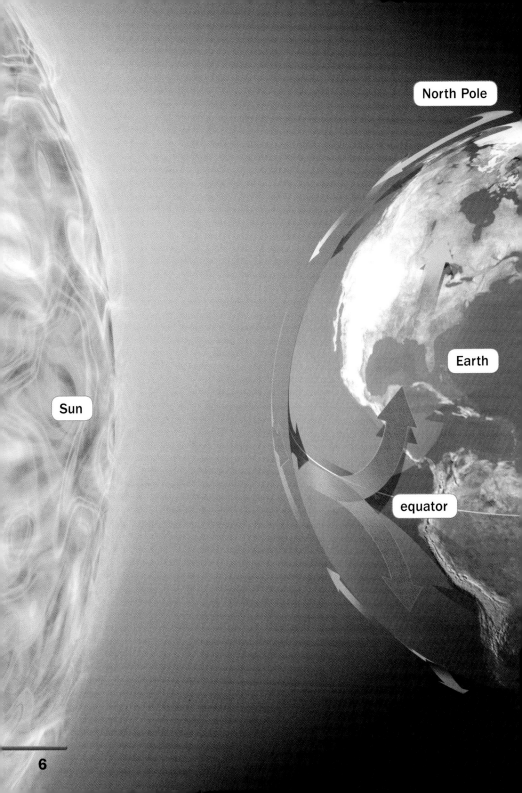

North Pole

Earth

Sun

equator

The weather depends on the movement of the earth, and the earth itself is a planet that is always changing and moving. Its atmosphere is like a vast weather engine—an engine that gets its power from the Sun.

The Sun heats up more air over the equator than it does at the poles. This causes huge movements of air across the surface of the earth. The warm, **moist**[1] air near the equator rises and flows toward the poles. The cool air from the poles then drops down and flows back toward the equator. This creates a continuous cycle of moving air.

---

[1] **moist:** slightly wet

Scan for Information

Scan page 7 to find the information.

1. Where does more air heat up?

2. What happens to the warm air?

3. What happens to the colder air?

4. What does this exchange of air create?

South Pole

As this air moves quickly across the earth's surface, it continuously interacts with the land and the sea. These components exchange heat and **moisture**[2], and create the earth's changing weather. That's why we get things like **heat waves**[3] and hailstorms, snowstorms and sandstorms, typhoons and tornados. All of these are types of extreme, or dramatic, weather.

Fronts can also cause dramatic weather, but what are they?

---

[2]**moisture:** small drops of water in the air
[3]**heat wave:** a period of unusually hot weather

Fronts are an important part of weather forecasts. Fronts are formed when warm air masses and cold air masses come together. These fronts can be cold or warm. A cold front is created when a mass of cold air forces itself underneath warmer, lighter air. The cold air pushes the warmer air out of the way. This often brings dramatic changes in the atmosphere, such as heavy clouds and violent storms.

Warm fronts happen when a warm air mass pushes cold air forward. The weather is usually less dramatic during warm fronts. It may get hotter and more **humid**[4], but rain and thunderstorms may also occur.

---

[4]**humid:** a kind of weather that is hot and slightly wet

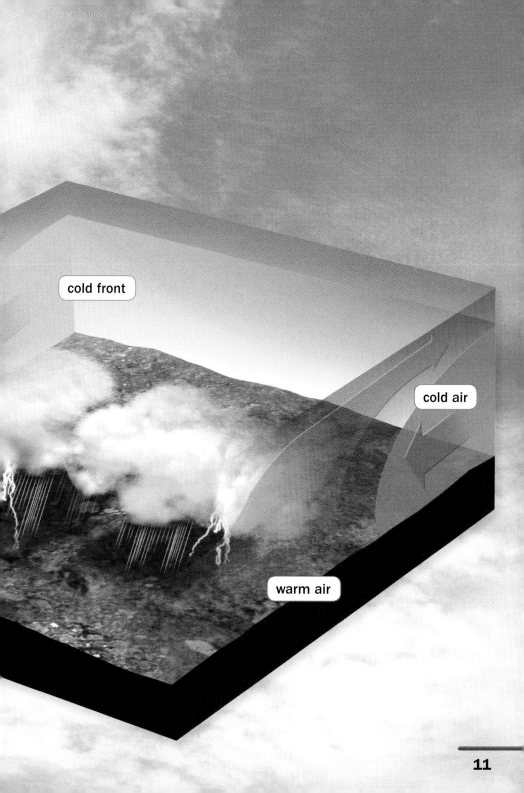

cold front

cold air

warm air

Scientists can often forecast tomorrow's weather by observing and analyzing the atmospheric conditions today. This science is called meteorology, and it's how the meteorologist on TV knows if you should pick up your umbrella, put on some sunglasses, or dress warmly.

Meteorologists, or weather forecasters, watch six key conditions of the atmosphere. These are: air pressure, or the weight of air above a certain point on the earth's surface; humidity, or the amount of moisture in the air; temperature; clouds; wind; and precipitation, such as rain or snow. Then, they try to make an accurate prediction of what the weather will be like tomorrow, or even next week.

Of course it's very useful to be able to know what the weather will be like in the future. But how is it done? Simple devices like **barometers**[5] and thermometers, or more complicated ones like radar and satellites, are used to measure weather conditions. This data is then used to predict all kinds of weather.

By measuring a rise in air pressure, for example, barometers can generally tell you to plan for nice weather. If the air pressure drops, there may be storms. Barometers are one way that you can forecast the weather for yourself, without the help of a meteorologist. Many people have them at home.

---

[5]**barometer:** an instrument that measures air pressure

Predict

Answer the questions. Then, scan page 17 to check your answers.

1. How many thunderstorms occur each day around the world?

2. In what order do these events happen during a thunderstorm? (Number 1-4)

_____ air cools and ice or water forms

_____ moisture gets heavy and falls to earth as rain

_____ humid air moves upward

_____ clouds form

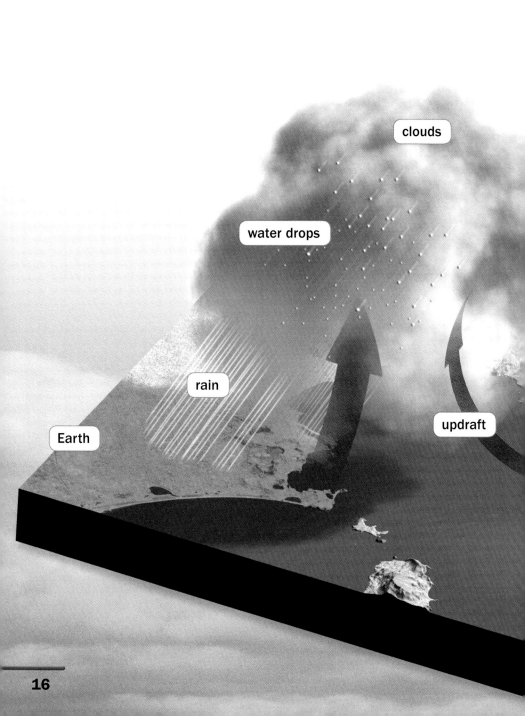

Thunderstorms are one of the most common forms of extreme weather. About 45,000 thunderstorms occur each day around the world. They usually begin with warm, humid air moving upward. This is called an 'updraft.' These updrafts rise above the earth and form clouds. Then, ice crystals or water drops form in the clouds as the air cools. Finally, this moisture becomes heavy and falls to the earth as rain.

However, it's not always just rain. If the air temperature is very cold, the moisture can become snow. It can also become hail or **sleet**[6], depending on the temperature.

———————————————

[6]**sleet:** frozen rain; a mixture of snow and rain

We may not always be happy about the weather, but everyone needs weather forecasts. They help us to plan our daily lives. Farmers depend on accurate forecasts to tell them when to plant and **harvest**[7] crops. Airlines need to consider weather conditions so that their planes can reach their destinations quickly and safely. And you? Well, a good understanding of the weather might help you to decide whether you should go out tomorrow... or not.

---

[7]**harvest:** gather fruits, vegetables, or other foods

After You Read

1. Weather can change at _____ time.
   A. no
   B. any
   C. the
   D. some

2. On page 4, the phrase 'temporary state' describes something that is:
   A. never changing
   B. always the same
   C. complex
   D. always changing

3. Which is NOT a part of the complex relationship that weather depends upon?
   A. air
   B. the Sun
   C. hailstorms
   D. water

4. On page 7, the word 'vast' is closest in meaning to:
   A. changing
   B. huge
   C. difficult
   D. hot

5. Which is an appropriate heading for page 9?
   A. Air
   B. Air Interacts with the Land and Sea
   C. Weather Is Dangerous
   D. Moisture Creates Earth's Changing Weather

6. On page 10, paragraph 2, 'it' refers to:
   A. the wind
   B. the rain
   C. a warm front
   D. the weather

7. Fronts are _____ important part of weather forecasts.

    A. two

    B. all

    C. an

    D. the

8. Which of the following is NOT used to measure weather?

    A. an umbrella

    B. a thermometer

    C. a satellite

    D. a radar

9. If air pressure rises, you will probably:

    A. pick up an umbrella

    B. put on a sweater

    C. put on sunglasses

    D. see hail

10. An appropriate heading for page 17 is:

    A. Thunderstorms Are Very Unusual

    B. How a Thunderstorm Happens

    C. How an Updraft Produces Good Weather

    D. How a Thunderstorm Causes an Updraft

11. Who depends on accurate weather forecasts?

    A. farmers

    B. airlines

    C. travelers

    D. all of the above

Global Warming

O ver time, the average temperature on the earth's surface constantly goes up and down. These changes are most often the result of differences in the amount of heat from the sun or natural changes in the atmosphere. It usually takes thousands of years for the temperature to change by even one degree Celsius. However, recent measurements show that the earth's temperature may have increased by almost this much in only the past 100 years. Some scientists believe that this rapid temperature change is the result of human, not natural, activity. The name for this kind of unusual change is global warming, and some scientists and meteorologists predict that it may cause serious problems around the world in the near future. Some even believe these problems are already beginning to happen.

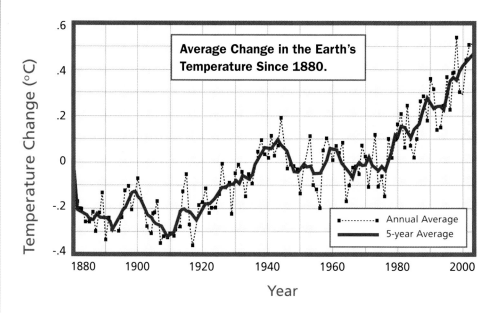

Average Change in the Earth's Temperature Since 1880.

- Annual Average
- 5-year Average

Temperature Change (°C)

Year

"One prediction is that by the year 2100, sea levels will be three feet higher than they are today."

While not all meteorologists and scientists agree that global warming is a reality, those who do agree have some serious concerns. They expect an increase in heat waves along with extremely heavy thunderstorms and floods in the near future. Some also predict that snowstorms will become more frequent and intense as global warming causes the level of moisture in the air to rise. In addition, others predict that the size and strength of hurricanes and typhoons will increase as the temperatures of the oceans rise.

These scientists also emphasize that people living in cities near the ocean or on small islands should be particularly concerned. They suggest that, as the earth's temperature increases, the ice at the north and south poles will begin to melt and cause sea levels to rise. This rise in the world's oceans will, in turn, cause coastal flooding. One prediction is that by the year 2100, sea levels will be three feet higher than they are today. This would mean that cities like Venice, Italy, and Miami, Florida, could lose significant amounts of land to the ocean. Although these are only predictions, the governments in most major countries are beginning to take them seriously.

CD 2, Track 10

Word Count: 329
Time: _____

Vocabulary List

atmosphere (2, 3, 7, 10, 12)
barometer (14)
earth (2, 3, 4, 7, 9, 12, 16)
equator (3, 7)
forecast (3, 12, 14, 18)
front (3, 9, 10)
hailstorm (2, 9, 17)
harvest (18)
heat wave (9)
humid (10, 12, 17)
meteorologist (3, 12, 14)
meteorology (3, 12)
moist (7)
moisture (9, 12, 17)
North Pole (3, 6)
planet (3, 7)
predict (3, 12, 14)
radar (3, 14)
sandstorm (2, 9)
satellite (3, 14)
sleet (17)
snowstorm (2, 9, 17)
South Pole (3)
thermometers (3, 14)
thunderstorm (2, 10, 17)
tornado (2, 9)
typhoon (2, 9)
weather condition (2, 14, 18)